THIS BOOK BELONGS TO:

_____

WELCOME TO HAWAII

Dedicated to all the explorers.

All rights reserved.
No part of this book may be reproduced in any form or by any means, electronic or mechanical, and no photocopying or recording, unless you have written permission from the author.

ISBN 978-1-958985-43-4

Text copyright © 2025 by Mimi Jones

www.joeysavestheday.com

A Mimi Book

HAWAII

The name "Hawaii" originates from the Hawaiian language, translating to "homeland." It is thought to derive from the native Hawaiian term "Owhyhee." The islands were first settled by Polynesians approximately 1,500 years ago.

Hawaii was the fiftieth state to join the Union.
It officially joined on August 21, 1959.

The state is made up of eight primary islands and is situated in the Pacific Ocean, to the southwest of the continental United States.

Hawaii is a territory of the United States; however, it is not physically connected to the mainland.

Honolulu is the capital of Hawaii.
It officially became the capital in 1845.

Honolulu, Hawaii, has an estimated population of about 350,420 people.

Hawaii ranks as the forty-seventh largest state in the United States and is regarded as a relatively small state.

Capital Building
415 S Beretania St
Honolulu, HI 96813

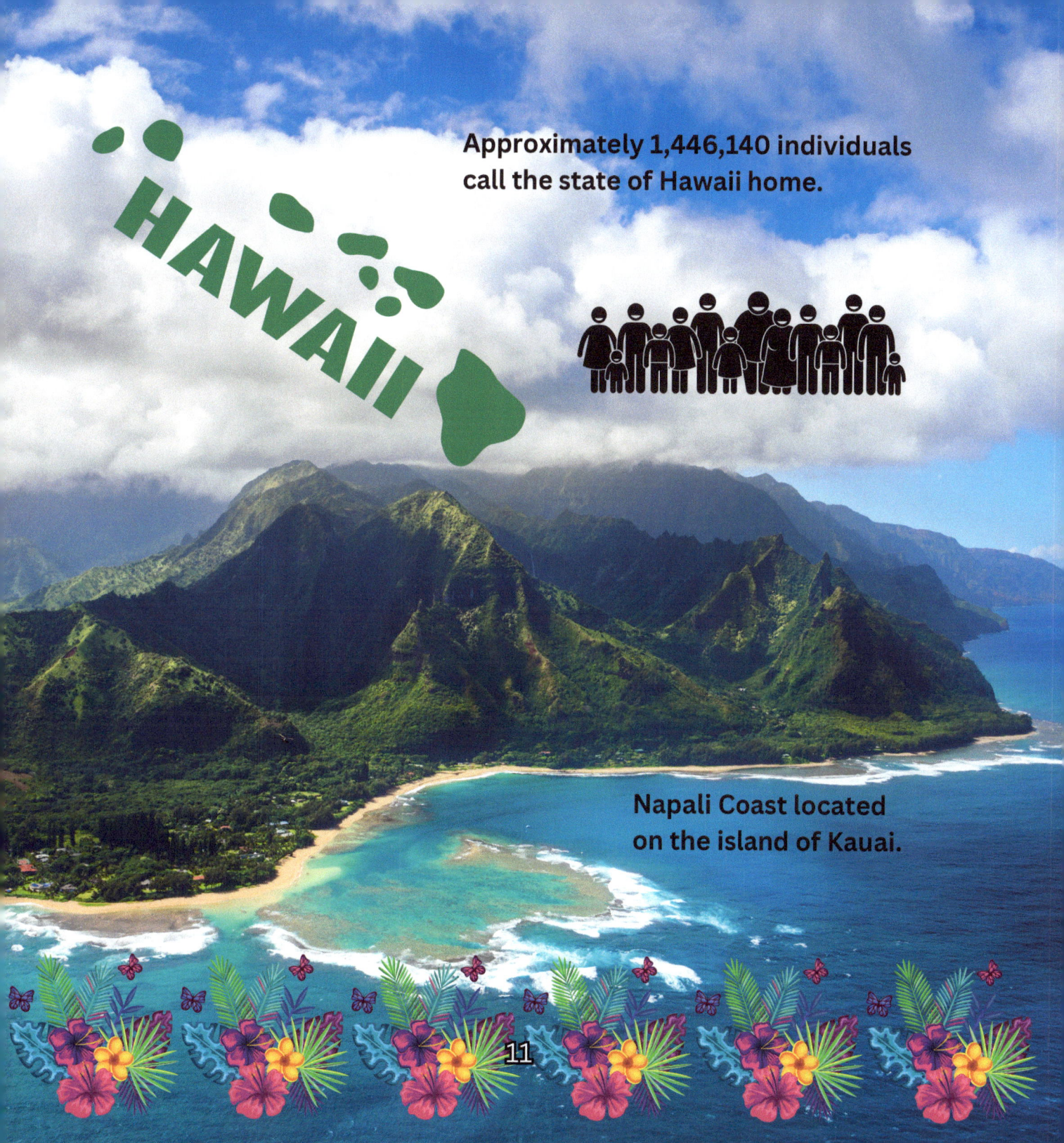

HAWAII

Approximately 1,446,140 individuals call the state of Hawaii home.

Napali Coast located on the island of Kauai.

Joseph Kekuku (1874–1932) was a talented Hawaiian musician credited with the invention of the steel guitar. He was born in Lāʻie, Oʻahu, where he first encountered the instrument's unique sound while studying at the Kamehameha School for Boys. Kekuku's groundbreaking work had a profound impact on American music, especially within the genres of country, blues, and rock 'n' roll.

Dr. Haunani-Kay Trask (1949-2021) was a respected Native Hawaiian scholar, teacher, and activist. She taught at the University of Hawai'i at Mānoa and started the Kamakakūokalani Center for Hawaiian Studies. Dr. Trask was dedicated to advocating for Native Hawaiian rights and independence. She authored books, poems, and films that showcased the challenges and strength of the Hawaiian community.

HAWAII

There are 5 counties in Hawaii.

Hawai'i County   Kalawao County   Maui County

Honolulu County   Kauai County

Molokini Crater, off the southwestern coast of Maui, is a crescent-shaped volcanic atoll known for its clear waters and rich marine life, ideal for snorkeling and diving. Nearby Turtle Town is famous for Hawaiian Green Sea Turtles, providing a captivating experience for visitors. Both locations embody Hawaii's underwater paradise, making them essential for ocean enthusiasts.

Hawaii is home to one of the world's most active volcanoes, Kilauea.

The islands have some of the world's best surfing spots, particularly on Oahu's North Shore.

Hawaii

The state fish is the Humuhumunukunukuapua'a, also known as the reef triggerfish.

18

ALOHA

The Aloha Tower, built in 1926, was once the tallest building in Hawaii.

The Nene, commonly referred to as the Hawaiian goose, was designated as Hawaii's state bird in 1957. This extraordinary bird is notable for its stunning appearance, characterized by a black head and a creamy tan chest. Its feathers boast intricate streaks of brown, white, and black on the underside, enhancing its allure.

The Hawaii official state flower is the yellow hibiscus. It became the state flower in 1988.

Hawaii is affectionately known by several nicknames, including Paradise, The Aloha State, and The Island of Aloha.

The state motto of Hawaii is "Ua Mau ke Ea o ka Aina i ka Pono," which means "The life of the land is perpetuated in righteousness." This motto was officially adopted on May 1, 1959.

THE LIFE OF THE

Hawaii's first official flag, adopted on December 29, 1845, symbolizes the islands' identity. It features eight horizontal stripes in red, blue, and white, representing the eight major islands: Hawai'i, Maui, O'ahu, Kaua'i, Moloka'i, Lāna'i, Ni'ihau, and Kaho'olawe. This distinctive design reflects Hawaii's rich history and unity.

Aloha

Hawaii boasts diverse agricultural products due to its unique climate and fertile soil. Key crops include:

- **Avocados:** Thrive in tropical conditions and are valued for their creamy texture and nutrition.
- **Kona Coffee:** Grown on the Big Island's slopes, known for its rich flavor from volcanic soil.
- **Pineapples:** Iconic to Hawaii, cultivated in large plantations for their sweetness.
- **Sugar Cane:** Historically significant to Hawaii's economy, used for local consumption and export.
- **Taro:** A traditional staple grown in wetland patches, essential for making poi, a popular dish.

These crops showcase Hawaii's rich agricultural diversity.

HAWAII

Hawaii's unique wildlife includes color-changing chameleons, playful dolphins, the native nene goose, and migrating humpback whales. These species enrich Hawaii's biodiversity.

Hawaii exhibits a diverse range of temperatures across the year. The highest temperature ever recorded in the state reached 100 degrees Fahrenheit in Pahala on April 27, 1931. On the other hand, the lowest temperature recorded was 12 degrees Fahrenheit at the Mauna Kea Observatory on May 17, 1979.

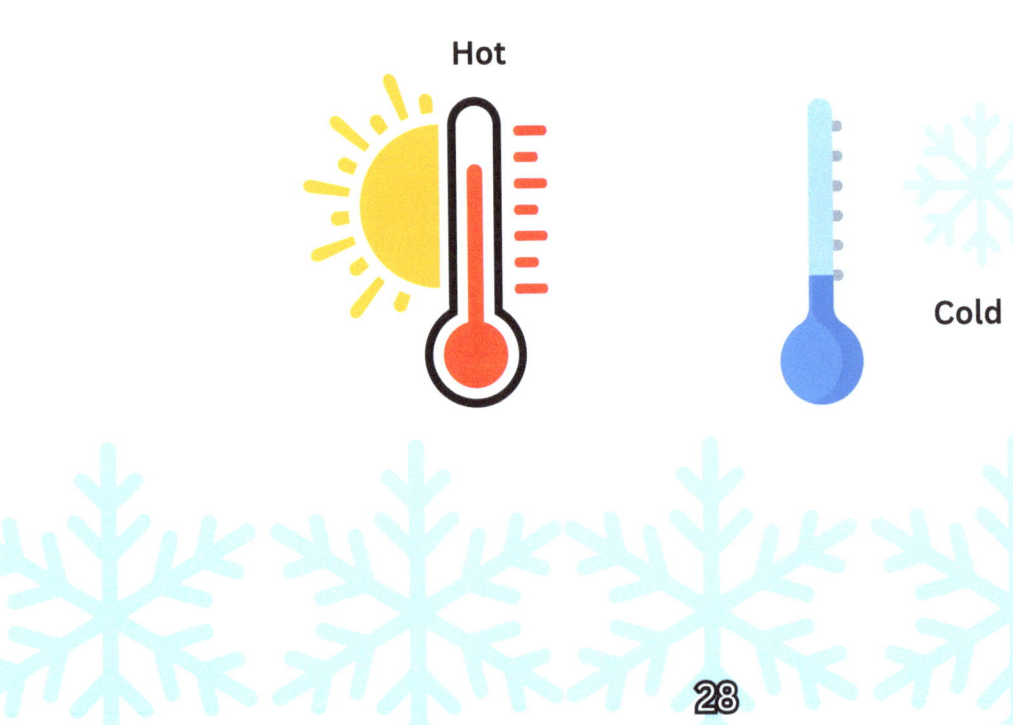

Hawaii has its own time zone called Hawaii-Aleutian Standard Time (HAST), and it doesn't observe daylight saving time.

Mauna Kea, a dormant volcano on the Big Island, is the tallest mountain in the world when measured from its base on the ocean floor.

   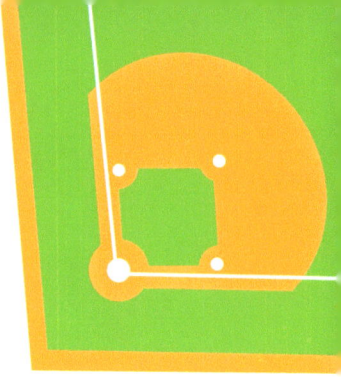

Hawaii is home to the Hawaii Islanders, a former minor-league baseball team that played from 1961 to 1987. Fans enjoyed watching games at Aloha Stadium in Honolulu, cheering for their local heroes. Baseball in Hawaii is a beloved sport, with young players dreaming of big league success. The warm climate and beautiful landscapes make it perfect for year-round play.

Hawaii's football team, the Rainbow Warriors, represents the University of Hawaii at Manoa. They play in the NCAA Division I, with home games at the Clarence T.C. Ching Athletics Complex in Honolulu. Football is a significant part of island culture, inspiring young athletes across Hawaii.

The USS Arizona Memorial in Pearl Harbor honors the lives lost during the attack on December 7, 1941.

Can you name these?

I hope you enjoyed learning about Hawaii.

To explore fun facts about the other 49 states, visit my website at www.joeysavestheday.com. You'll also find a wide variety of homeschool resources to support joyful learning at home. If you enjoyed this book, I would be grateful if you left a review. Your feedback truly helps. Thank you for your support!

Check out these other interesting books in the 50 States Fact Books Series!

www.mimibooks.com